Book and CDs for B♭, E♭, C and Bass Clef Instruments

BOOK




Cover Photo: Alberto Romeu

ISBN 978-1-4234-9713-4

DISTRIBUTED BY

7777 W. BLUEMOUND RD. P.O. BOX 13819 MILWAUKEE, WI 53213





**www.boosey.com**
**www.halleonard.com**

CDs

| TITLE | CD Track Number Split Track/Melody | CD Track Number Full Stereo Track |
|---|---|---|
| **CD1** | | |
| **Brazil Blues** | 1 | 2 |
| **Brussels in the Rain** | 3 | 4 |
| **Impressions of Tiananmen Square** | 5 | 6 |
| **The Magic City (Miami)** | 7 | 8 |
| **Samba for Carmen** | 9 | 10 |
| **CD2** | | |
| **Snow Samba** | 1 | 2 |
| **Song for Maura** | 3 | 4 |
| **Song to My Son** | 5 | 6 |
| **To Brenda with Love** | 7 | 8 |
| **Who's Smokin'?** | 9 | 10 |

## Paquito D'Rivera

***Paquito D'Rivera*** (clarinets, winds) is an award-winning composer, conductor, performer, and author. Born in Havana, Cuba, D'Rivera performed at age 10 with the National Theater Orchestra, studied at the Havana Conservatory, and, at 17, became a featured soloist with the Cuban National Symphony. An intrepid explorer in the global musical landscape, Paquito has written and conducted works for full orchestra (for the Rotterdam Philharmonic and the National Symphony Orchestra, among others), played with and conducted big bands (Dizzy Gillespie's United Nations Orchestra), written and performed chamber music (with Yo-Yo Ma, the Assad Brothers), and concertized with every combination of instrumental group. Awards include the Jazz Masters Award from the NEA and the National Medal of the Arts, Honorary Doctorates from the University of Pennsylvania and Berklee College of Music, the Frankfurter Musikpreis, a Guggenheim Fellowship in Music Composition, and the President's Award from the International Association for Jazz Education. The winner of nine NARAS GRAMMY® awards, Paquito D'Rivera is the Artistic Director of the Festival Internacional de Jazz de Punte del Este in Uruguay and the DC Jazz Festival (formerly the Duke Ellington Jazz Festival) in Washington, D.C., as well as Composer-in-Residence at the Caramoor Center for Music and the Arts, with the Orchestra of St. Luke's.

# PAQUITO D'RIVERA BRAZILIAN JAZZ

**Volume 113**

**Featured Players:**

**Paquito D'Rivera–Clarinet and Saxes**
**Diego Urcola–Trumpet and Valve Trombone**
**Danilo Perez–Piano**
**Sergio Brandão–Bass**
**Portinho–Drums**
**Edson "Café" Da Silva–Percussion**

**All tracks recorded at Freiberg Music Studios, Ardsley, New York**
**Horn overdubs and mix by Daniel Freiberg**

## HOW TO USE THE CD:

Each song has two tracks:

**1) Melody and Solo**

Use this track as a learning tool for melody style and inflection.

**2) Backing Tracks**

Learn and perform with this accompaniment track with the RHYTHM SECTION only.

CD I

1 : WITH HORNS
2 : BACKING TRACKS

C VERSION

# BRAZIL BLUES

PAQUITO D'RIVERA

MEDIUM LATIN
SOLOS (25 CHORUSES)

# BRUSSELS IN THE RAIN

CD 1

5 : WITH HORNS
6 : BACKING TRACKS

C VERSION

# IMPRESSIONS OF TIANANMEN SQUARE

PAQUITO D'RIVERA

CD I
7 : WITH HORNS
8 : BACKING TRACKS
C VERSION
THE MAGIC CITY (MIAMI)
PAQUITO D'RIVERA
ARRANGED BY
C. FRANZETTI
SAMBA CANÇÃO
RHYTHM
PLAY 3 CHORUSES
2ND X
1ST X
LAST X TO CODA
CODA
1ST X ONLY
REPEAT AND FADE

CD I

9 : WITH HORNS
10 : BACKING TRACKS

# SAMBA FOR CARMEN

PAQUITO D'RIVERA

C VERSION

MEDIUM SAMBA

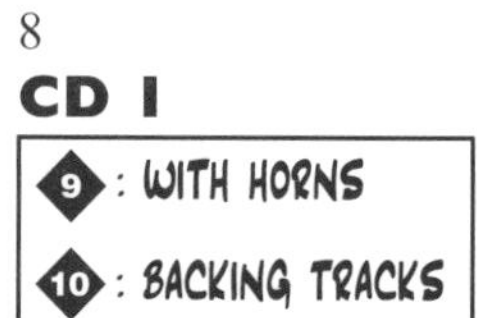

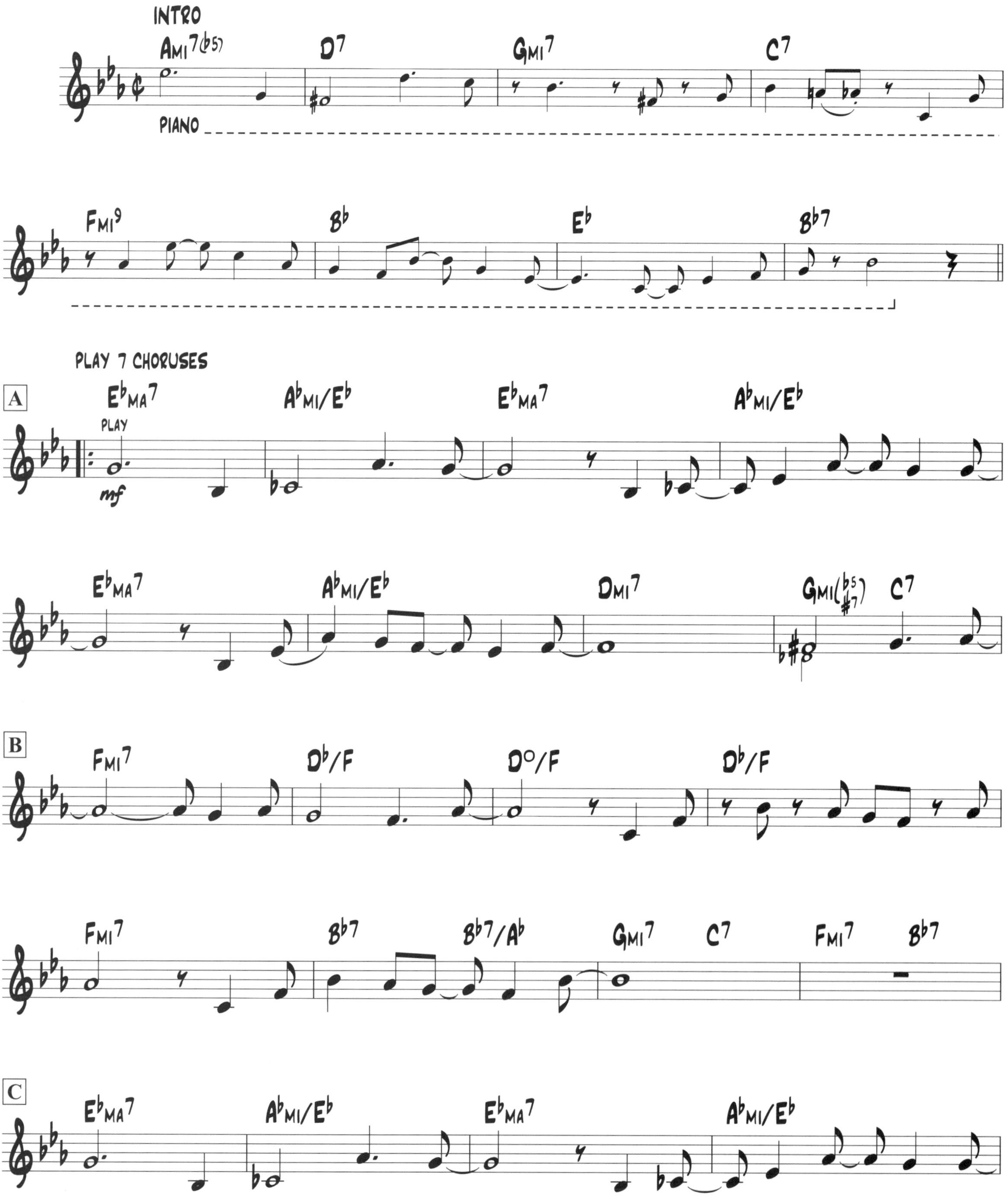

INTRO
AMI7(b5)
D7
GMI7
C7
PIANO
FMI9
Bb
Eb
Bb7
PLAY 7 CHORUSES
A
EbMA7
PLAY
mf
AbMI/Eb
EbMA7
AbMI/Eb
EbMA7
AbMI/Eb
DMI7
GMI(b5 #7)
C7
B
FMI7
Db/F
D°/F
Db/F
FMI7
Bb7
Bb7/Ab
GMI7
C7
FMI7
Bb7
C
EbMA7
AbMI/Eb
EbMA7
AbMI/Eb

E♭MA7
E♭7
A♭MA7
D
AMI7(♭5)
D7
G7
C7(♭9)
FMI7
B♭7
E♭MA7
E♭7
E
AMI7(♭5)
D7
GMI7
C7
LAST X TO CODA
FMI7
B♭7
E♭
B♭7
CODA
AMI7(♭5)
A♭7
E♭/G
G♭7
FMI7
EMA7
F/E♭

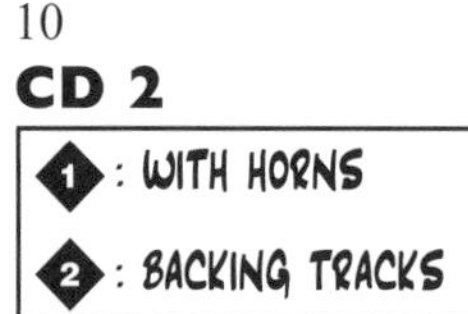


# SNOW SAMBA

C VERSION

PAQUITO D'RIVERA
AND CLAUDIO RODITI

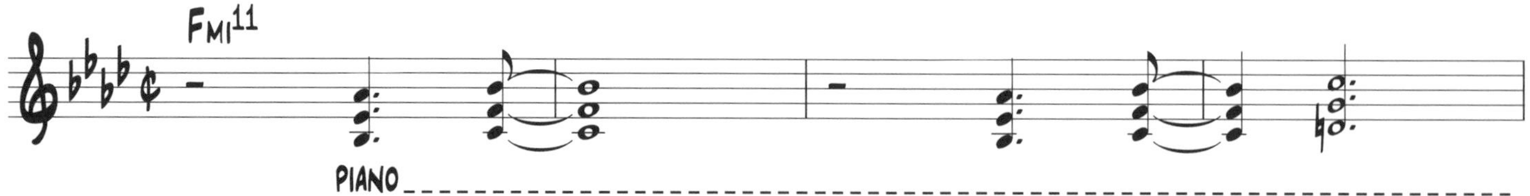


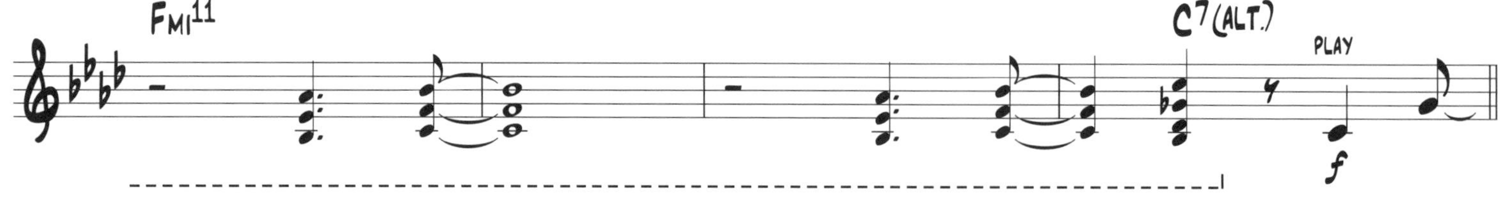

C
C7(b9)
FMA7/C
GMI7/C
FMA7/C
GMI7/C
BMI7(b5)
E7(#9)
AMI7
D7(b9)
GMI7
C7
CMI7
F7
BMI7(b5)
E7(#9)
AMI7
D7(b9)
GMI7
C7
D
FMI11
FMI11
D.S. AND FADE
C7(ALT.)

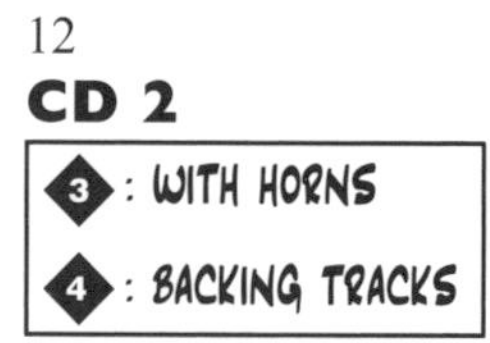

CD 2

3 : WITH HORNS

4 : BACKING TRACKS

# SONG FOR MAURA

PAQUITO D'RIVERA

C VERSION

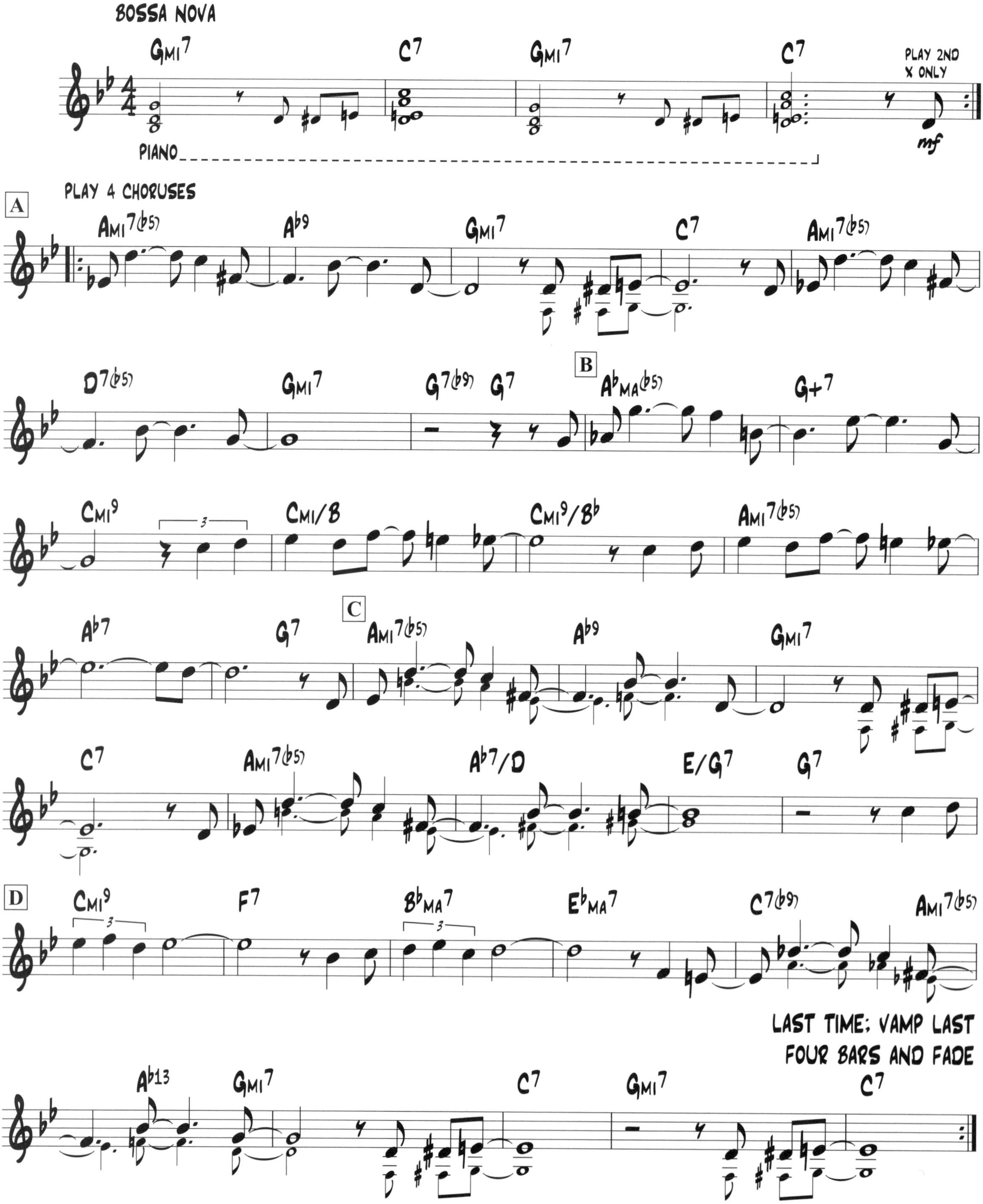

BOSSA NOVA
GMI7 C7 GMI7 C7
PLAY 2ND X ONLY
mf
PIANO
PLAY 4 CHORUSES
A
AMI7(♭5) A♭9 GMI7 C7 AMI7(♭5)
D7(♭5) GMI7 G7(♭9) G7
B
A♭MA(♭5) G+7
CMI9 CMI/B CMI9/B♭ AMI7(♭5)
3
A♭7 G7
C
AMI7(♭5) A♭9 GMI7
C7 AMI7(♭5) A♭7/D E/G7 G7
D
CMI9 F7 B♭MA7 E♭MA7 C7(♭9) AMI7(♭5)
LAST TIME: VAMP LAST FOUR BARS AND FADE
A♭13 GMI7 C7 GMI7 C7

CD 2

5 : WITH HORNS
6 : BACKING TRACKS

C VERSION

# SONG TO MY SON

PAQUITO D'RIVERA

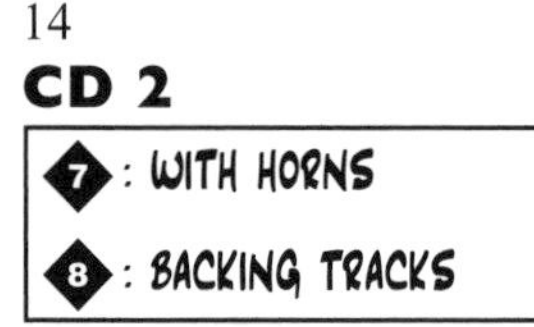


# TO BRENDA WITH LOVE

PAQUITO D'RIVERA

C VERSION

D
G7
CMA9
F7(13/9)
CMA7
Bb7
E
A7
DMI9
G7
EbMI7
Ab7
EMI7
A7
A/G
F#MI
C7(13)
B7
DMI7
G7
F
CMA9
CMI9
CMA9
TO CODA
CMI9
CODA
REPEAT AND FADE
CMA9
CMI9

CD 2

9 : WITH HORNS

10 : BACKING TRACKS

C VERSION

# WHO'S SMOKIN'?

PAQUITO D'RIVERA
AND CLAUDIO RODITI

CD 2
9 : WITH HORNS
10 : BACKING TRACKS

# WHO'S SMOKIN'?

PAQUITO D'RIVERA
AND CLAUDIO RODITI

Bb VERSION

CD I

1 : WITH HORNS
2 : BACKING TRACKS

# BRAZIL BLUES

PAQUITO D'RIVERA

Bb VERSION

MEDIUM LATIN
SOLOS (25 CHORUSES)

CD I

3 : WITH HORNS

4 : BACKING TRACKS

# BRUSSELS IN THE RAIN

PAQUITO D'RIVERA

CD I

5 : WITH HORNS
6 : BACKING TRACKS

Bb VERSION

# IMPRESSIONS OF TIANANMEN SQUARE

PAQUITO D'RIVERA

CD I
7 : WITH HORNS
8 : BACKING TRACKS
THE MAGIC CITY (MIAMI)
Bb VERSION
PAQUITO D'RIVERA
ARRANGED BY
C. FRANZETTI
SAMBA CANÇÃO
RHYTHM
PLAY 3 CHORUSES
A
B
C
2ND X
1ST X
LAST X TO CODA
CODA
1ST X ONLY
REPEAT AND FADE

CD I

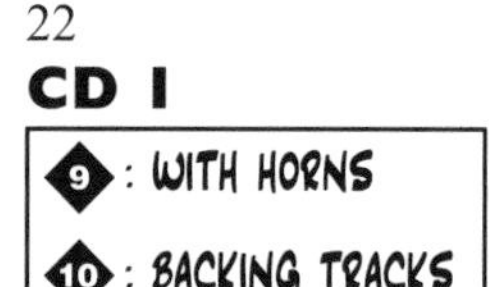


# SAMBA FOR CARMEN

PAQUITO D'RIVERA

MEDIUM SAMBA
INTRO

PLAY 7 CHORUSES

FMA7
F7
B♭MA7
D
BMI7(♭5)
E7
A7
D7(♭9)
GMI7
C7
FMA7
F7
E
BMI7(♭5)
E7
AMI7
D7
LAST X TO CODA
GMI7
C7
F
C7
CODA
BMI7(♭5)
B♭7
F/A
A♭7
GMI7
F♯MA7
G/F

CD 2

1 : WITH HORNS
2 : BACKING TRACKS

# SNOW SAMBA

B♭ VERSION

PAQUITO D'RIVERA
AND CLAUDIO RODITI

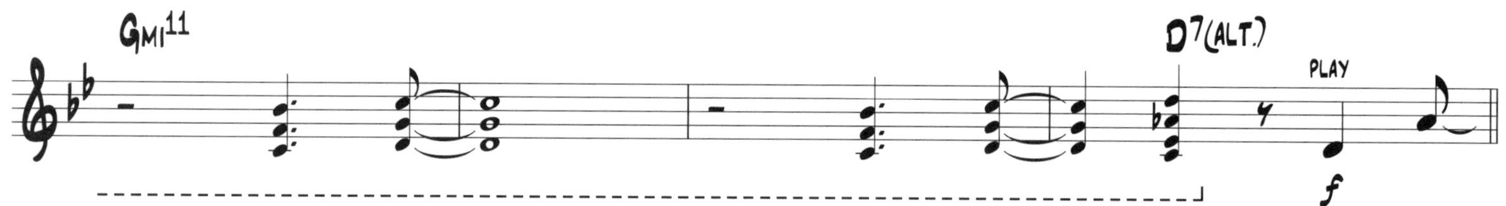

C
D7(b9)
GMA7/D
AMI7/D
GMA7/D
AMI7/D
C#MI7(b5)
F#7(#9)
BMI7
E7(b9)
AMI7
D7
DMI7
G7
C#MI7(b5)
F#7(#9)
BMI7
E7(b9)
AMI7
D7
D
GMI11
D.S. AND FADE
GMI11
D7(ALT.)

**CD 2**

: WITH HORNS
: BACKING TRACKS

# SONG FOR MAURA

PAQUITO D'RIVERA

B♭ VERSION

BOSSA NOVA

AMI7 D7 AMI7 D7

PLAY 2ND X ONLY

*mf*

PIANO

A PLAY 4 CHORUSES

BMI7(♭5) B♭9 AMI7 D7 BMI7(♭5)

E7(♭5) AMI7 A7(♭9) A7 B B♭MA(♭5) A+7

DMI9 DMI/C♯ DMI9/C BMI7(♭5)

B♭7 A7 C BMI7(♭5) B♭9 AMI7

D7 BMI7(♭5) B♭7/E F♯/A7 A7

D DMI9 G7 CMA7 FMA7 D7(♭9) BMI7(♭5)

LAST TIME; VAMP LAST FOUR BARS AND FADE

B♭13 AMI7 D7 AMI7 D7

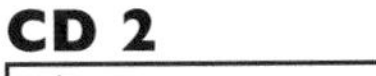


5 : WITH HORNS

6 : BACKING TRACKS

# SONG TO MY SON

PAQUITO D'RIVERA

Bb VERSION

SLOW SAMBA CANÇÃO
PLAY 3 CHORUSES

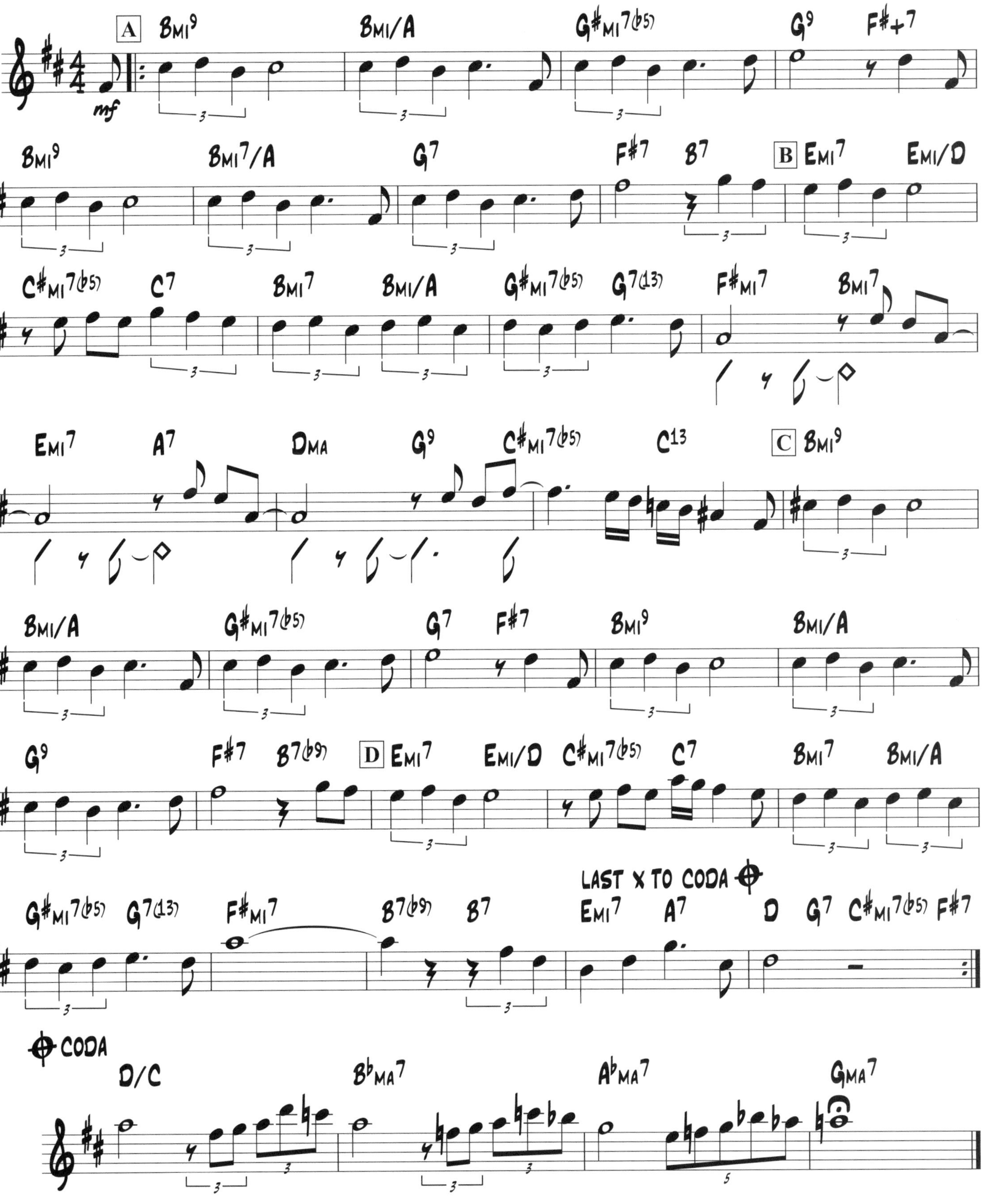

A  BMI9 | BMI/A | G#MI7(b5) | G9 F#+7

BMI9 | BMI7/A | G7 | F#7 B7 | B EMI7 EMI/D

C#MI7(b5) C7 | BMI7 BMI/A | G#MI7(b5) G7(13) | F#MI7 BMI7

EMI7 A7 | DMA G9 | C#MI7(b5) C13 | C BMI9

BMI/A | G#MI7(b5) | G7 F#7 | BMI9 | BMI/A

G9 | F#7 B7(b9) | D EMI7 EMI/D | C#MI7(b5) C7 | BMI7 BMI/A

LAST X TO CODA

G#MI7(b5) G7(13) | F#MI7 | B7(b9) B7 | EMI7 A7 | D G7 C#MI7(b5) F#7

CODA

D/C | BbMA7 | AbMA7 | GMA7

CD 2

7 : WITH HORNS
8 : BACKING TRACKS

Bb VERSION

# TO BRENDA WITH LOVE

PAQUITO D'RIVERA

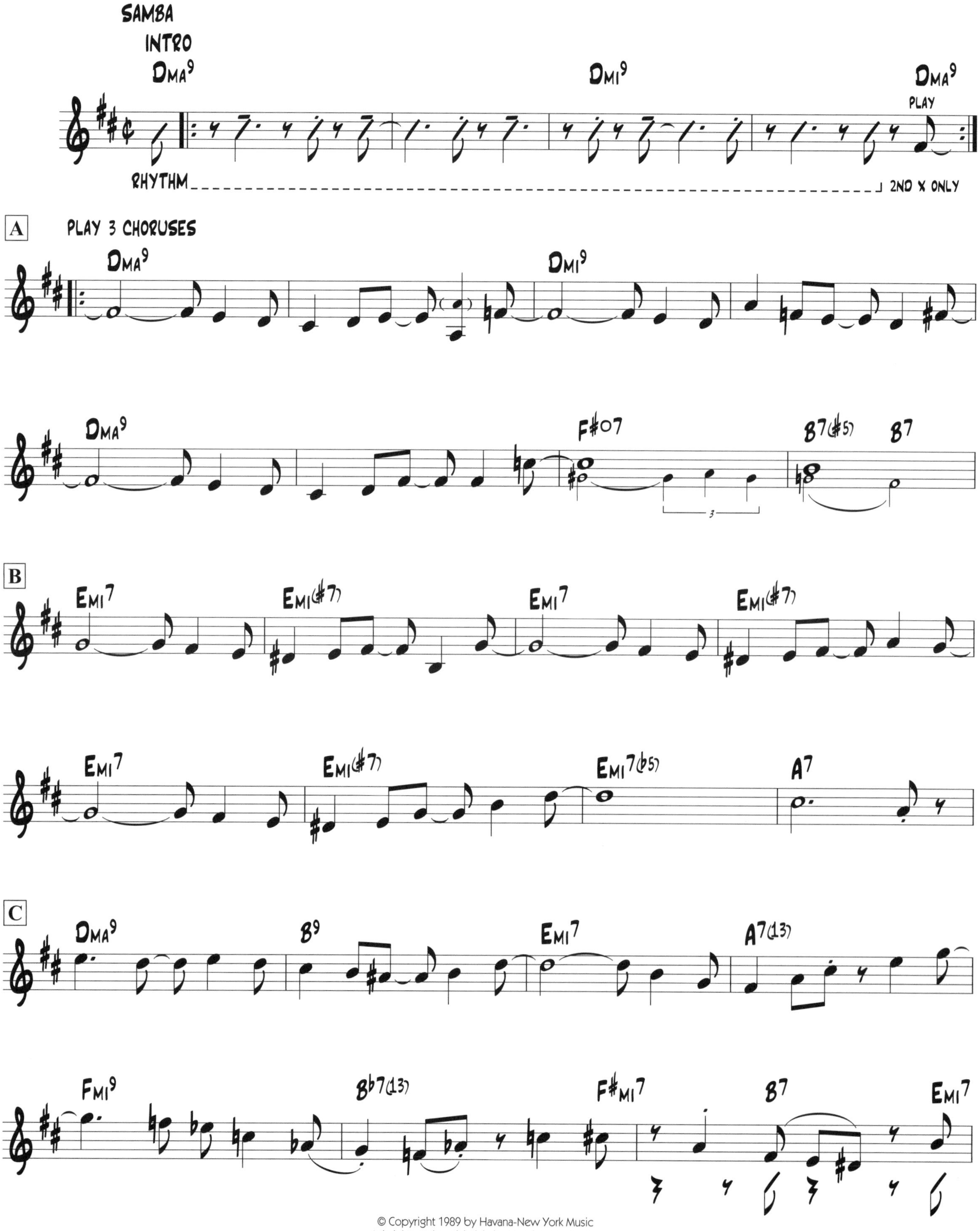
SAMBA
INTRO
DMA9
DMI9
DMA9
PLAY
RHYTHM
2ND X ONLY
A
PLAY 3 CHORUSES
DMA9
DMI9
DMA9
F#07
B7(#5)
B7
B
EMI7
EMI(#7)
EMI7
EMI(#7)
EMI7
EMI(#7)
EMI7(b5)
A7
C
DMA9
B9
EMI7
A7(13)
FMI9
Bb7(13)
F#MI7
B7
EMI7

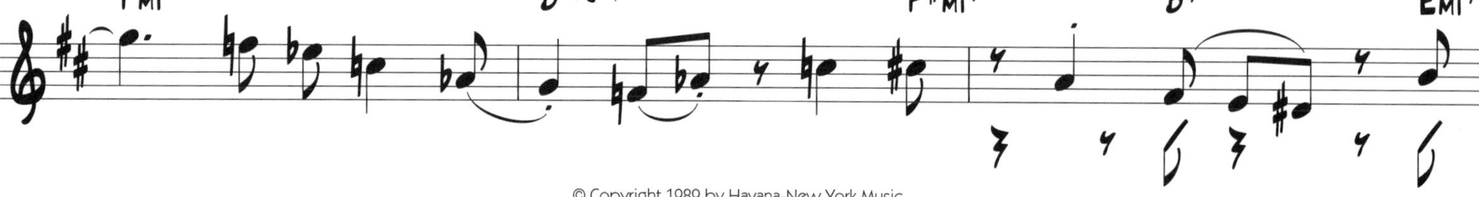

D
A7
DMA9
G7(13 9)
DMA7
C7
3
B7
E
EMI9
A7
FMI7
Bb7
F#MI7
B7
B/A
G#MI
D7(13)
C#7
EMI7
A7
F
DMA9
DMI9
DMA9
TO CODA
DMI9
CODA
REPEAT AND FADE
DMA9
DMI9

CD I

1 : WITH HORNS

2 : BACKING TRACKS

Eb VERSION

# BRAZIL BLUES

PAQUITO D'RIVERA

MEDIUM LATIN

SOLOS (25 CHORUSES)

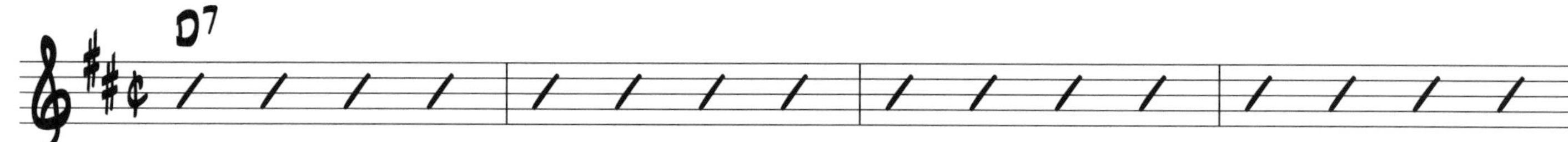

CD I

3 : WITH HORNS
4 : BACKING TRACKS

# BRUSSELS IN THE RAIN

PAQUITO D'RIVERA

Eb VERSION

CD 1

5: WITH HORNS
6: BACKING TRACKS

# IMPRESSIONS OF TIANANMEN SQUARE

PAQUITO D'RIVERA

CD I
7 : WITH HORNS
8 : BACKING TRACKS
THE MAGIC CITY (MIAMI)
Eb VERSION
PAQUITO D'RIVERA
ARRANGED BY
C. FRANZETTI
SAMBA CANÇÃO
RHYTHM
PLAY 3 CHORUSES
A
B
C
2ND X
1ST X
LAST X TO CODA
CODA
1ST X ONLY
REPEAT AND FADE

CD 1

9: WITH HORNS
10: BACKING TRACKS

# SAMBA FOR CARMEN

PAQUITO D'RIVERA

INTRO

PLAY 7 CHORUSES

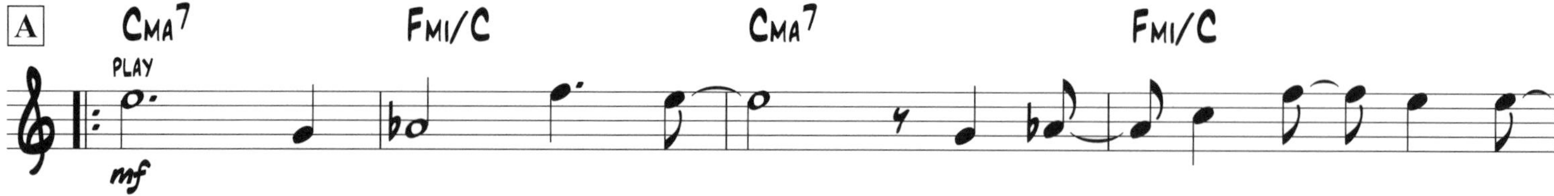

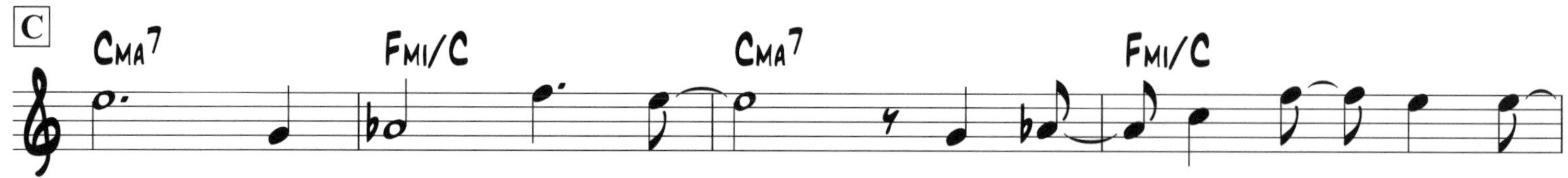

CMA7
C7
FMA7
D
F#MI7(b5)
B7
E7
A7(b9)
DMI7
G7
CMA7
C7
E
F#MI7(b5)
B7
EMI7
A7
LAST X TO CODA
DMI7
G7
C
G7
CODA
F#MI7(b5)
F7
C/E
Eb7
DMI7
C#MA7
D/C

CD 2

# SNOW SAMBA

Eb VERSION

PAQUITO D'RIVERA
AND CLAUDIO RODITI

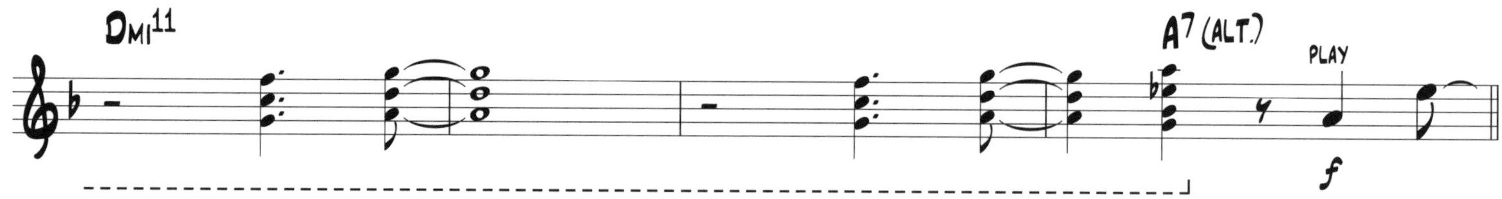

C
A7(♭9)
DMA7/A
EMI7/A
DMA7/A
EMI7/A
G♯MI7(♭5)
C♯7(♯9)
F♯MI7
B7(♭9)
EMI7
A7
AMI7
D7
G♯MI7(♭5)
C♯7(♯9)
F♯MI7
B7(♭9)
EMI7
A7
D
DMI11
DMI11
D.S. AND FADE
A7 (ALT.)

**CD 2**

3 : WITH HORNS
4 : BACKING TRACKS

# SONG FOR MAURA

PAQUITO D'RIVERA

E♭ VERSION

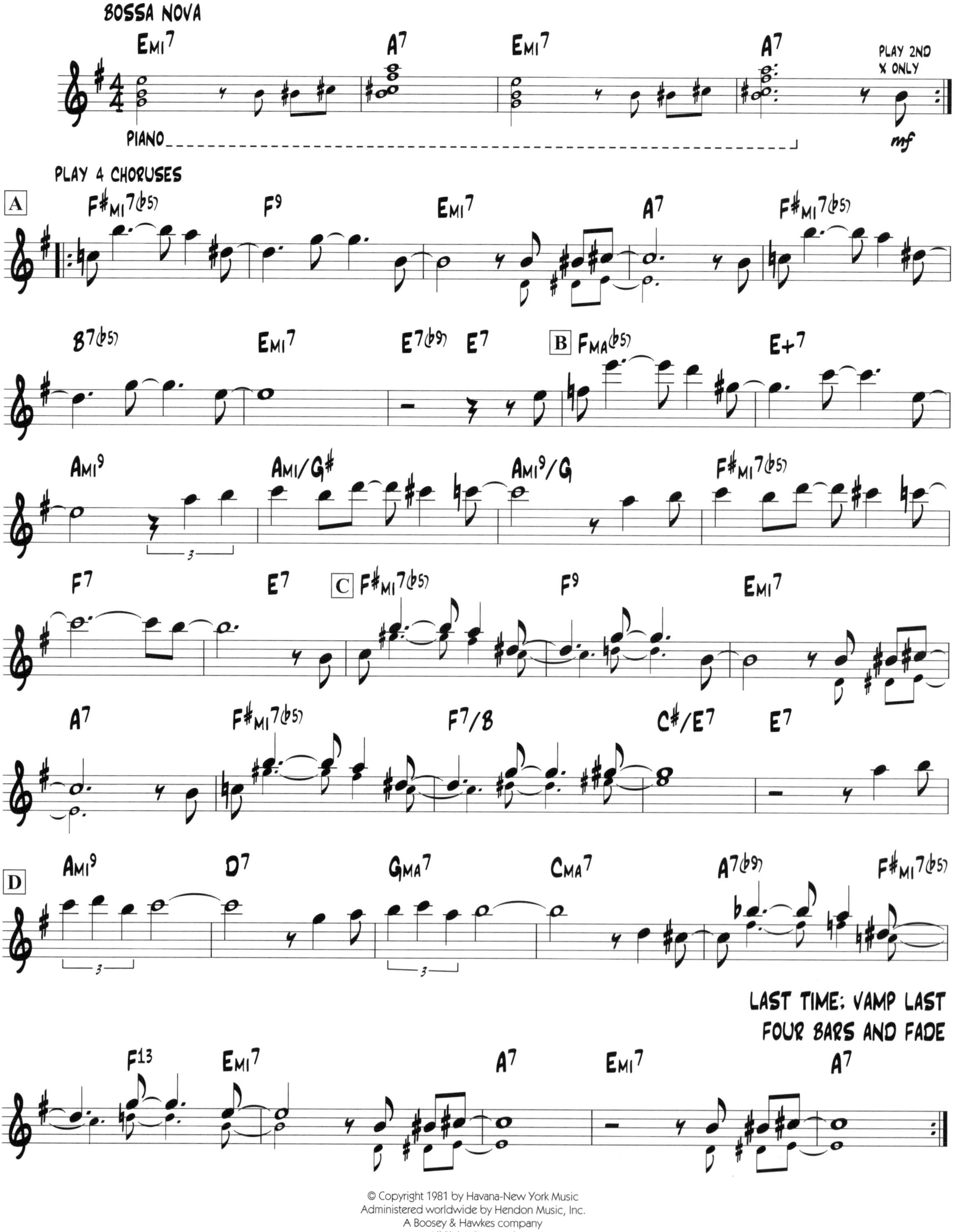

BOSSA NOVA

EMI7 A7 EMI7 A7

PLAY 2ND X ONLY

PIANO

*mf*

PLAY 4 CHORUSES

A F♯MI7(♭5) F9 EMI7 A7 F♯MI7(♭5)

B7(♭5) EMI7 E7(♭9) E7 B FMA(♭5) E+7

AMI9 AMI/G♯ AMI9/G F♯MI7(♭5)

3

F7 E7 C F♯MI7(♭5) F9 EMI7

A7 F♯MI7(♭5) F7/B C♯/E7 E7

D AMI9 D7 GMA7 CMA7 A7(♭9) F♯MI7(♭5)

3 3

LAST TIME; VAMP LAST FOUR BARS AND FADE

CD 2

5 : WITH HORNS

6 : BACKING TRACKS

Eb VERSION

# SONG TO MY SON

PAQUITO D'RIVERA

CD 2

7 : WITH HORNS
8 : BACKING TRACKS

# TO BRENDA WITH LOVE

PAQUITO D'RIVERA

E♭ VERSION

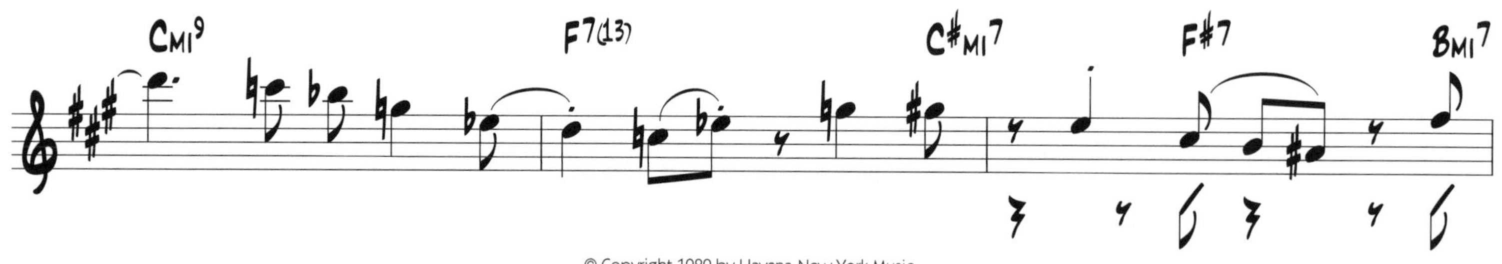

D
E7
AMA9
D7(13 9)
AMA7
G7
E
F#7
BMI9
E7
CMI7
F7
C#MI7
F#7
F#/E
D#MI
A7(13)
G#7
BMI7
E7
F
AMA9
AMI9
AMA9
TO CODA
AMI9
CODA
AMA9
AMI9
REPEAT AND FADE

CD 2

9 : WITH HORNS

10 : BACKING TRACKS

# WHO'S SMOKIN'?

PAQUITO D'RIVERA
AND CLAUDIO RODITI

# WHO'S SMOKIN'?

CD 2

9 : WITH HORNS

10 : BACKING TRACKS

C VERSION

PAQUITO D'RIVERA
AND CLAUDIO RODITI

FAST BAIÃO
PLAY 6 FULL CHORUSES

A

B♭7 E♭7 B♭7

FMI7 B♭7 E♭7 E°7

B♭7 G+7 CMI7

F7 B♭7 A♭7 A7 B♭7 A♭7 1. A7 B♭7 F7

B 2. A7 B♭7 G+7 SAMBA CMI7 F7(♯5) B♭MA7 G+7

CMI7 F+7 B♭MA7 EMI7(♭5) A7

DMI7 A/G CMI7 G/F

E♭MI7 A♭7 D♭MA7 CMI7 F7

CD I

1 : WITH HORNS

2 : BACKING TRACKS

𝄢 C VERSION

# BRAZIL BLUES

PAQUITO D'RIVERA

MEDIUM LATIN

SOLOS (25 CHORUSES)

F7

CD 1

# BRUSSELS IN THE RAIN

PAQUITO D'RIVERA

CD 1

5 : WITH HORNS
6 : BACKING TRACKS

C VERSION

# IMPRESSIONS OF TIANANMEN SQUARE

PAQUITO D'RIVERA

CD I
7 : WITH HORNS
8 : BACKING TRACKS
C VERSION
THE MAGIC CITY (MIAMI)
PAQUITO D'RIVERA
ARRANGED BY
C. FRANZETTI
SAMBA CANÇÃO
RHYTHM
PLAY 3 CHORUSES
mf
2ND X
1ST X
LAST X TO CODA
CODA
1ST X ONLY
REPEAT AND FADE

**CD I**

9 : WITH HORNS

10 : BACKING TRACKS

# SAMBA FOR CARMEN

PAQUITO D'RIVERA

C VERSION

PLAY 7 CHORUSES

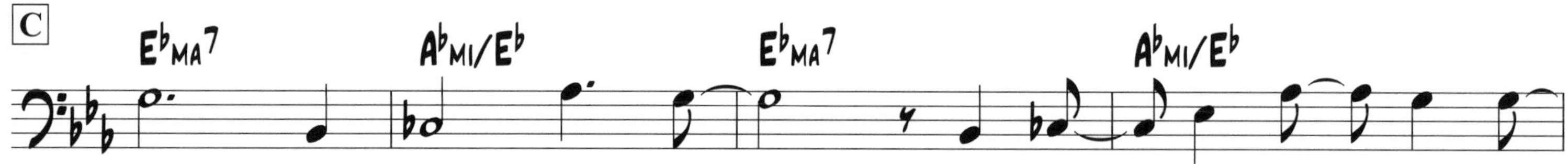

E♭MA7
E♭7
A♭MA7

D
AMI7(♭5)
D7
G7
C7(♭9)

FMI7
B♭7
E♭MA7
E♭7

E
AMI7(♭5)
D7
GMI7
C7

LAST X TO CODA
FMI7
B♭7
E♭
B♭7

CODA
AMI7(♭5)
A♭7
E♭/G
G♭7


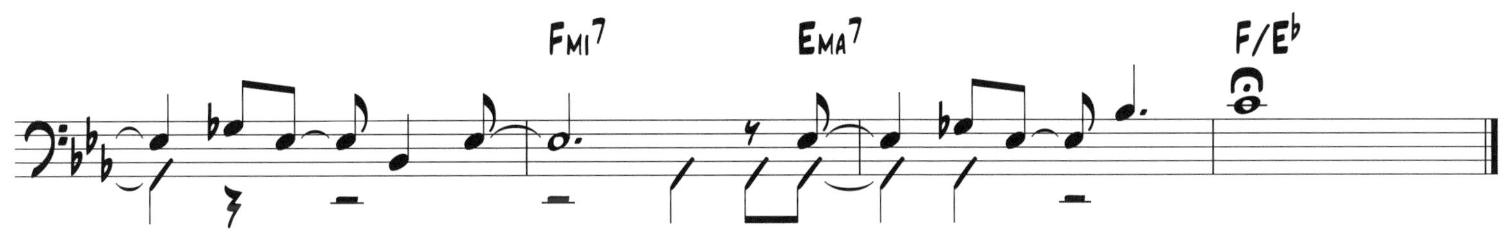

FMI7
EMA7
F/E♭

**CD 2**

| | |
|---|---|
| 1 | : WITH HORNS |
| 2 | : BACKING TRACKS |

# SNOW SAMBA

PAQUITO D'RIVERA
AND CLAUDIO RODITI

𝄢 C VERSION

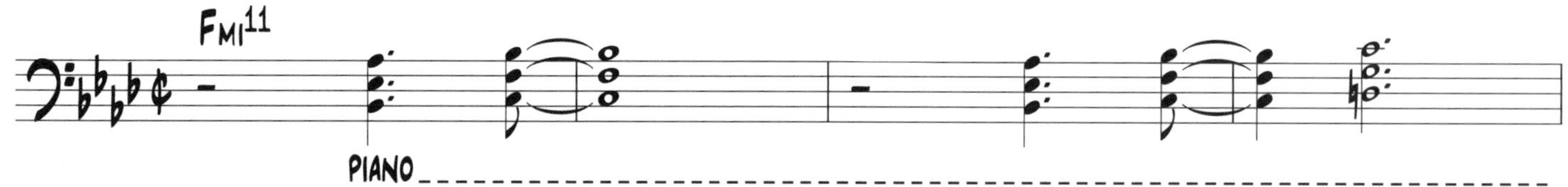


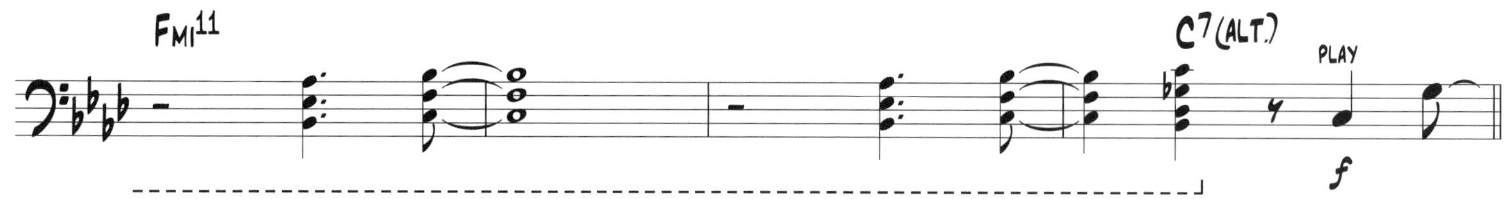

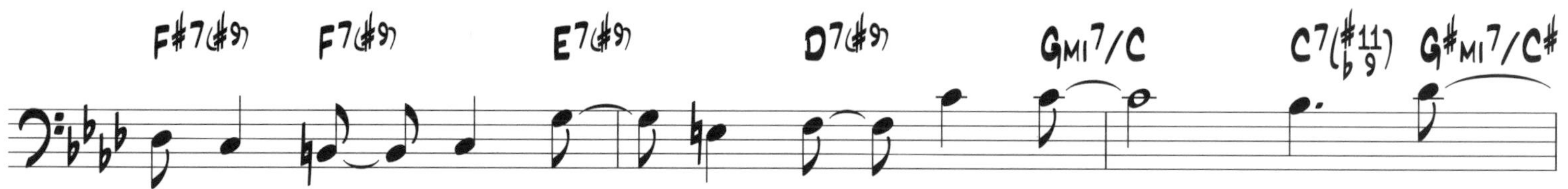

C
C7(b9)
FMA7/C
GMI7/C
FMA7/C
GMI7/C
BMI7(b5)
E7(#9)
AMI7
D7(b9)
GMI7
C7
CMI7
F7
BMI7(b5)
E7(#9)
AMI7
D7(b9)
GMI7
C7
D
FMI11
D.S. AND FADE
FMI11
C7(ALT.)

**CD 2**

3 : WITH HORNS

4 : BACKING TRACKS

# SONG FOR MAURA

PAQUITO D'RIVERA

BOSSA NOVA

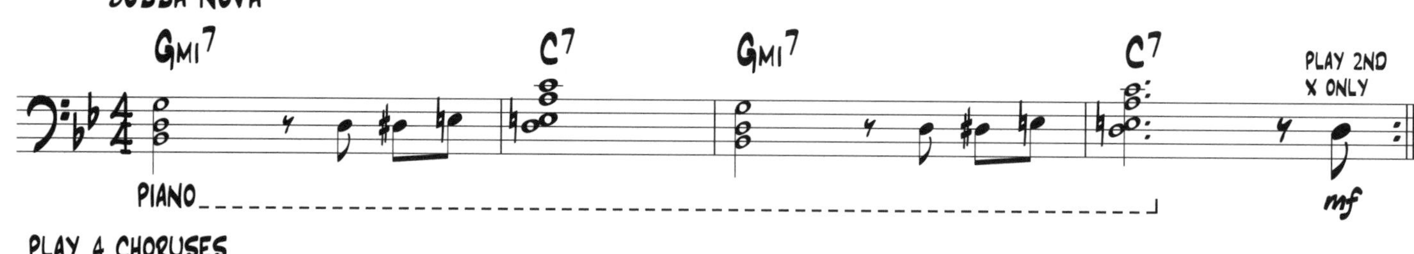


PLAY 4 CHORUSES

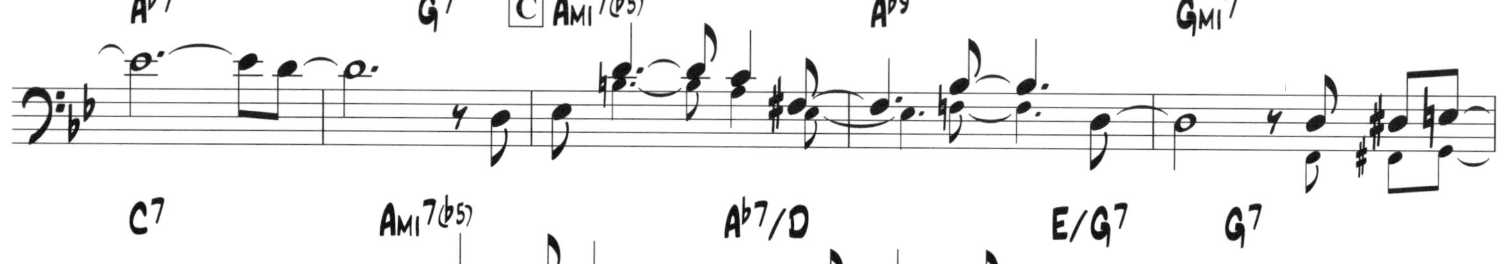

LAST TIME; VAMP LAST FOUR BARS AND FADE

CD 2

5 : WITH HORNS
6 : BACKING TRACKS

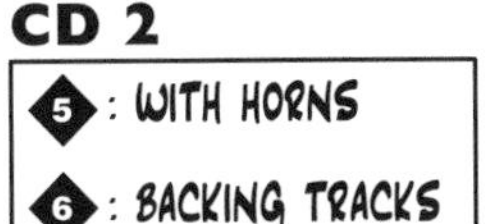

# SONG TO MY SON

PAQUITO D'RIVERA

C VERSION

SLOW SAMBA CANÇÃO
PLAY 3 CHORUSES

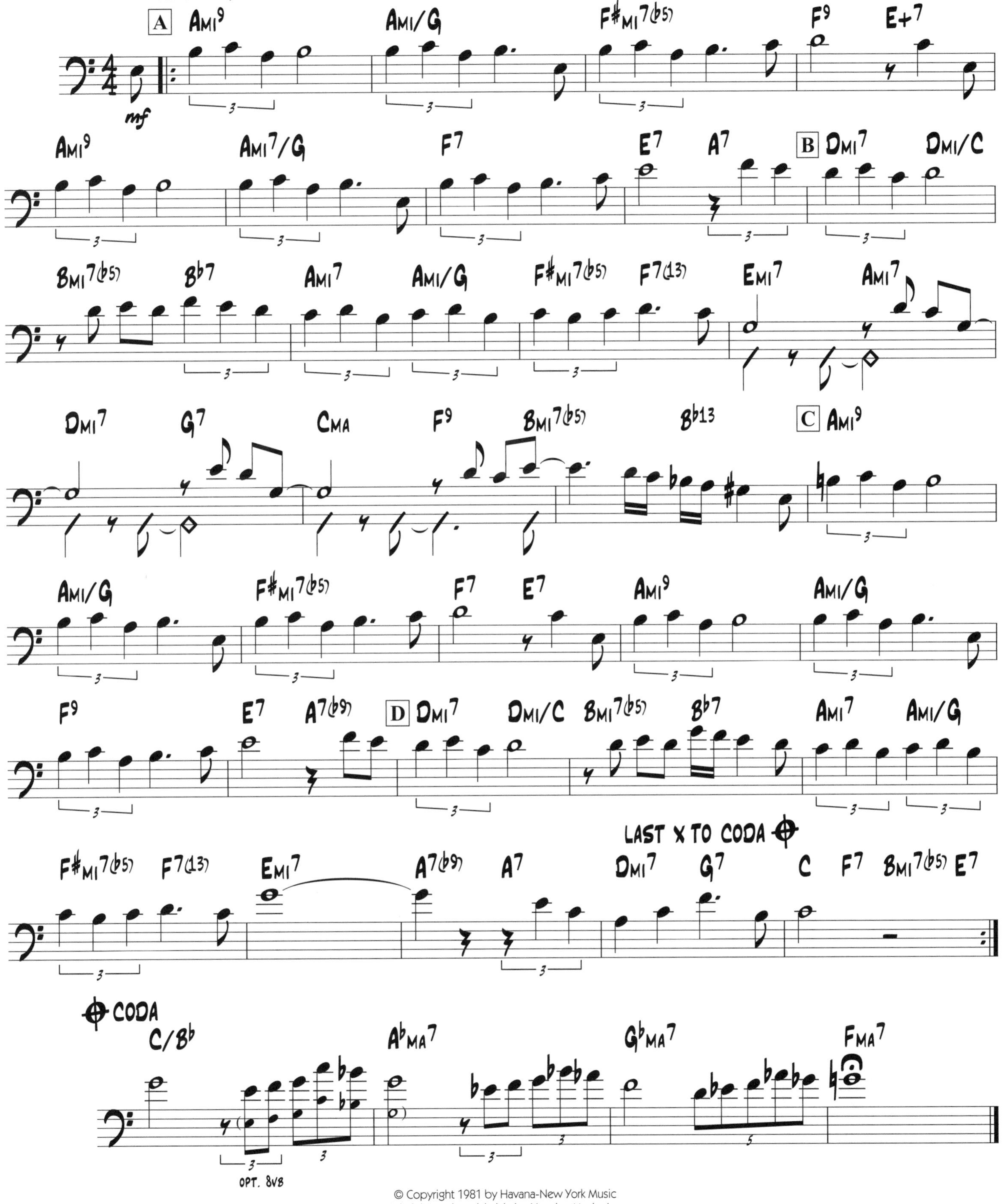

A AMI9 AMI/G F#MI7(♭5) F9 E+7
mf
AMI9 AMI7/G F7 E7 A7 B DMI7 DMI/C
BMI7(♭5) B♭7 AMI7 AMI/G F#MI7(♭5) F7(13) EMI7 AMI7
DMI7 G7 CMA F9 BMI7(♭5) B♭13 C AMI9
AMI/G F#MI7(♭5) F7 E7 AMI9 AMI/G
F9 E7 A7(♭9) D DMI7 DMI/C BMI7(♭5) B♭7 AMI7 AMI/G
LAST X TO CODA
F#MI7(♭5) F7(13) EMI7 A7(♭9) A7 DMI7 G7 C F7 BMI7(♭5) E7
CODA
C/B♭ A♭MA7 G♭MA7 FMA7
OPT. 8VB

CD 2

7 : WITH HORNS

8 : BACKING TRACKS

# TO BRENDA WITH LOVE

PAQUITO D'RIVERA

C VERSION

SAMBA

INTRO

A PLAY 3 CHORUSES

B

C

D
G7
CMA9
F7(13 9)
CMA7
B♭7
E
A7
DMI9
G7
E♭MI7
A♭7
EMI7
A7
A/G
F♯MI
C7(13)
B7
DMI7
G7
F
CMA9
CMI9
CMA9
CMI9
TO CODA
CODA
CMA9
CMI9
REPEAT AND FADE